CASTLE
AT WAR
THE STORY
OF A SIEGE

Setting up the
siege engines

Wall crenellations

Storing food
in the keep

A prisoner in the
dungeons

Releasing the arm
of a trebuchet

Hunting crossbow,
1450-1470

CASTLE
AT WAR
THE STORY OF A SIEGE

Written by
ANDREW LANGLEY

Illustrated by
PETER DENNIS

Longbow
made from yew
wood

DORLING KINDERSLEY
LONDON • NEW YORK • MOSCOW • SYDNEY

The Enemy Appr

> "When they heard that they were about to be besieged, they had the alarm bells rung and ordered that everyone should arm himself for the defence of the town."
>
> *Froissart's Chronicles* for 1342

TROUBLE WAS NOT LONG i
Three days after the lor
arrived at the gatehouse wit
The lord's neighbour, a pow
heading for the castle with a
siege weapons.

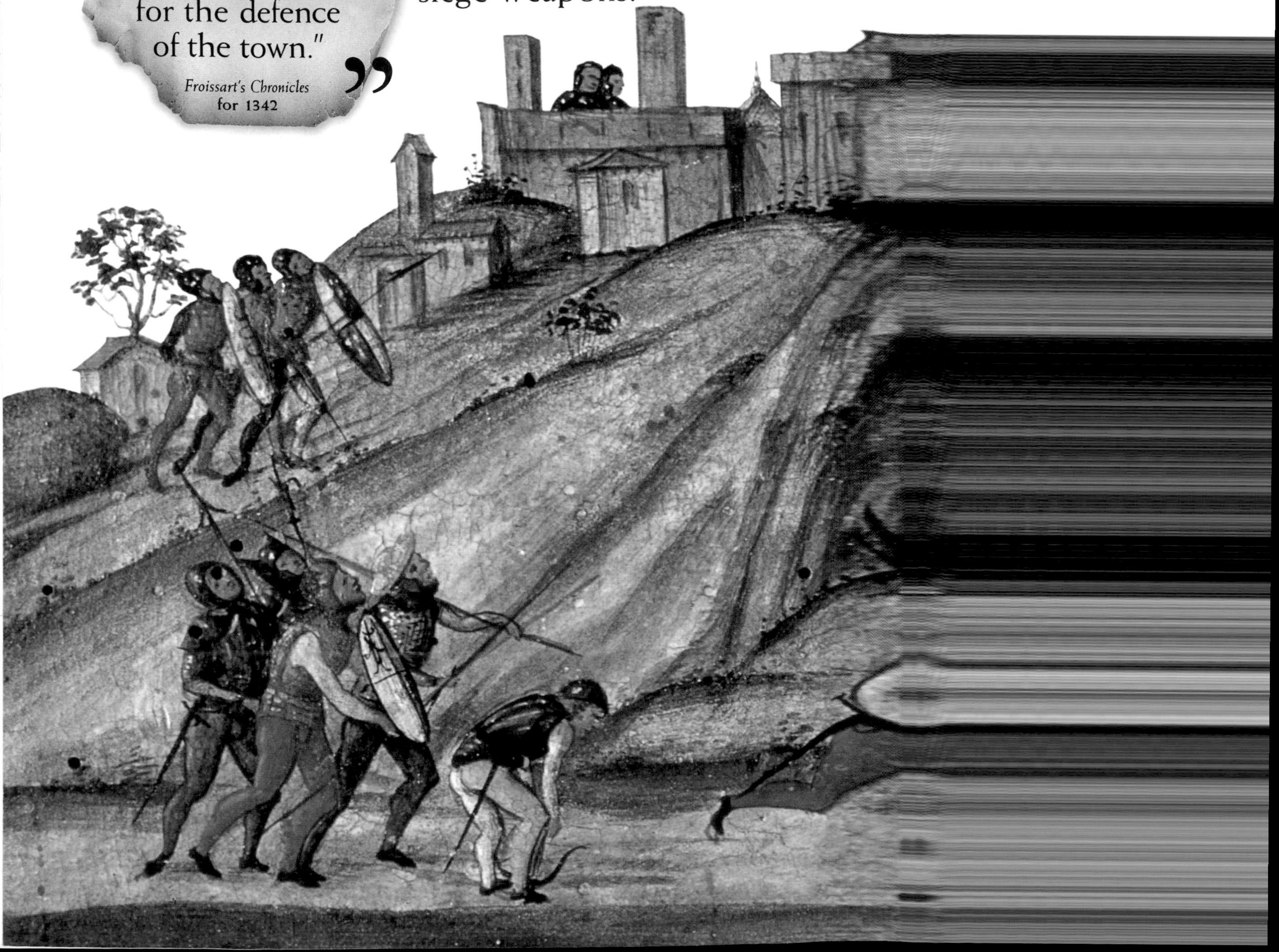

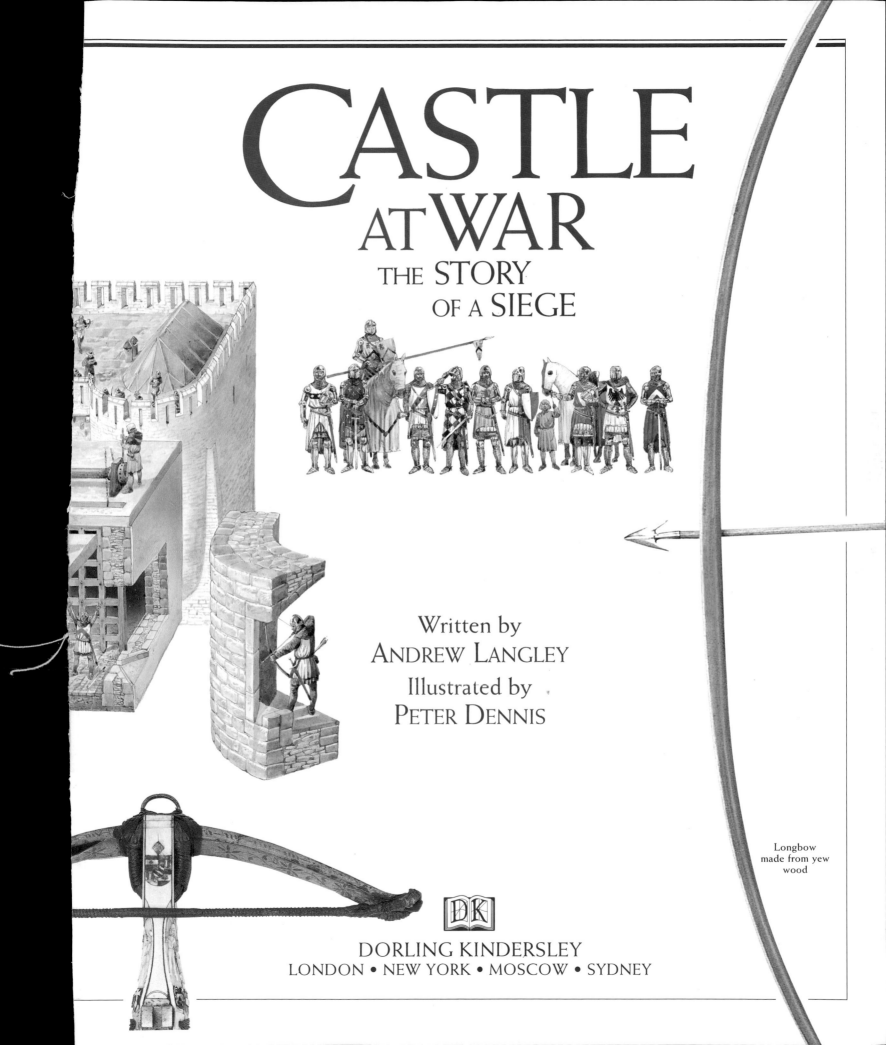

CASTLE
AT WAR
THE STORY
OF A SIEGE

Written by
ANDREW LANGLEY

Illustrated by
PETER DENNIS

Longbow
made from yew
wood

DORLING KINDERSLEY
LONDON • NEW YORK • MOSCOW • SYDNEY

A DORLING KINDERSLEY BOOK

Senior Editor Scarlett O'Hara
Senior Art Editor Vicky Wharton
Visualisation Dorian Spencer Davies
Senior Managing Editor Linda Martin
Senior Managing Art Editor Julia Harris
DTP Designer Almudena Díaz
Picture Research Catherine Edkins
Jacket Designer Mark Haygarth
Production Lisa Moss
Consultant Christopher Gravett

First published in 1998
by Dorling Kindersley Limited,
9 Henrietta Street, Covent Garden,
London WC2E 8PS

2 4 6 8 10 9 7 5 3 1

A CIP catalogue record for this book is available
from the British Library

ISBN 0 7513 5802 9

Reproduced by Colourscan, Singapore
Printed and bound by L.E.G.O., Italy

Additional illustrations by John Lawrence and
Venice Shone

Contents

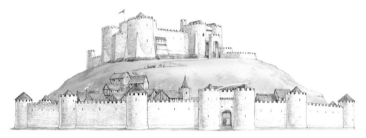
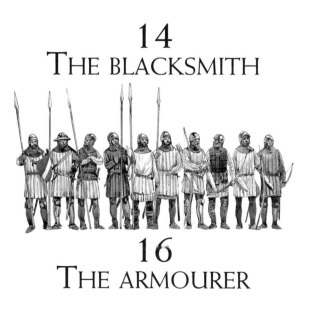

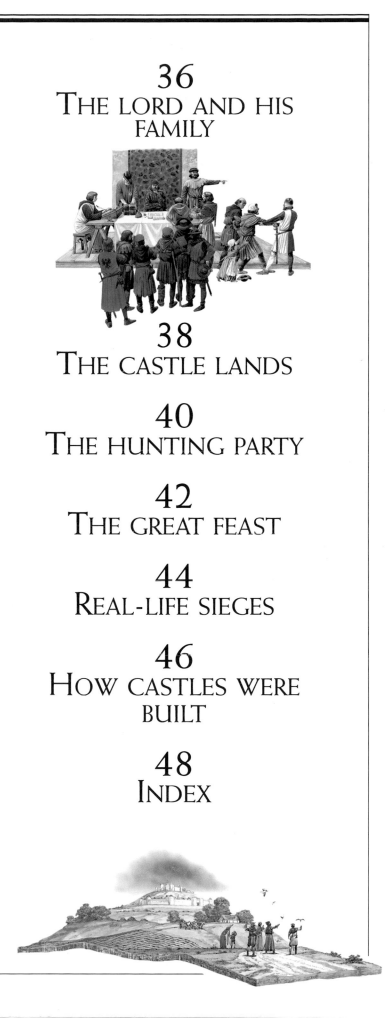

THE STORY OF CASTLES

THE CASTLE STOOD ON THE TOP OF a hill. With its massive towers and tall, windowless walls, it dominated the landscape. From high on the castle keep, a lookout could see for miles in all directions. Just below the castle lay the town, protected by its own walls and towers. Beyond the town walls, fields and woods stretched away into the distance. There were thousands of similar castles scattered all over Europe during the Middle Ages. Each was a king or nobleman's home and the fortified base where he kept his garrison of mounted knights and men-at-arms. From his castle, he could go out to defend his own lands or attack his neighbour's lands.

OUR CASTLE

Our castle has been here for a long time. The keep (the tallest part of the castle) was built in 1150. A century later, it was surrounded by thick walls with a round tower at each corner and the castle's main rooms inside. A century after that, an outer wall was built with extra stables and workshops.

FACT file

- Over 10,000 castles were built in Germany, 10,000 in France, and 2,000 in Britain and Ireland.
- A castle controlled territory for about 16 km (10 miles) all around it – as far as a knight could ride in a day.
- King Edward I of England spent £80,000 on castle building in Wales (about £25 million today).
- Castles in some low-lying areas were protected by water-filled moats. On a hill, there was not enough water.

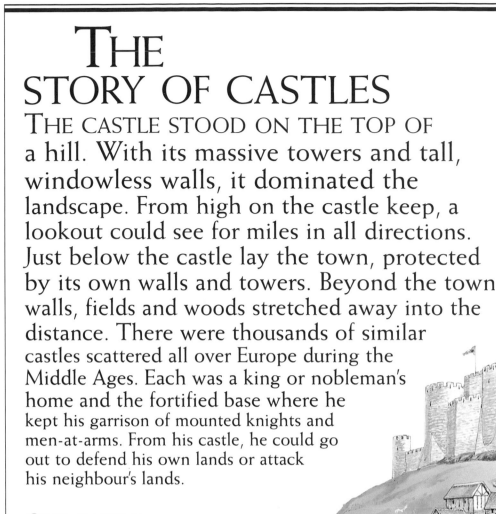

KEEPING THE ENEMY OUT
The barbican was an extra fortification projecting from the outer wall. From here, bowmen could shoot at people attacking the gatehouse.

BEHIND THE WALL
The houses in the town were built mostly of timber and mud. But the strong town wall around them was made from stone.

LOCKED UP
The two town gates, one on the north and one on the south side of the castle, were locked at dusk.

How castles developed

IN IRON AGE TIMES, people built forts on hill tops. They dug a ditch around the hill and heaped the earth into ramparts (banks) to keep enemies out. Communities lived inside the earthworks. By the 10th century, lords were using the idea for their own fortified houses – the first castles.

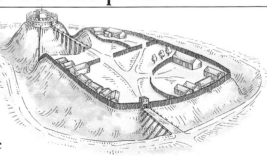

Motte and bailey
An early kind of castle was a wooden tower built on a flat-topped mound, or motte, with a wooden palisade (fence) around it. A guarded gateway and bridge led to a larger enclosed area, the bailey.

Tower keep
By the 11th century, some towers were built of stone, which was both fireproof and much stronger than wood. In the 13th century, a stone curtain wall with a large gatehouse surrounded this massive keep or great tower.

A tunnel through the cliff led to the castle's only entrance.

Defenders on the rock could easily pick off an enemy on the causeway.

Pleshey town within its defences

Motte of rammed earth above the castle bailey

CLIFF-TOP STRONGHOLD

Castle builders tried to find sites that were difficult to attack. Dunnottar Castle in Scotland (shown above) was built on a vast rock that jutted out into the North Sea. The sheer sides of the rock were impossible to climb. An attacking army could approach only along the narrow strip of land connecting the rock with the coast.

Castle and village
At Pleshey, in England, the motte and bailey were protected by a moat. The moat was extended to enclose a town that grew up at the same time as the castle.

An enemy soldier crossing the open space around the castle made an easy target.

The hard rock of the hill discouraged attackers from mining (digging underneath) the walls.

MARKET TOWN
The town grew up here because of the castle, which provided security and a market for the goods produced in the town.

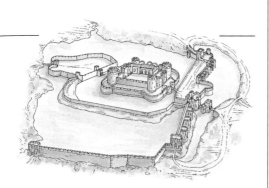

Concentric castle
By the 13th century, many new castles had no keep at all. Increasingly, the buildings inside were protected by two sets of curtain walls, the outer one lower than the inner. These are called concentric castles.

THE KING AND HIS PEOPLE
The king sat at the pinnacle of medieval society. He granted areas of land, or fiefs, to his most powerful subjects – the barons (top left), the bishops (top right), and the lesser nobles (bottom). They built their castles on the land they had been given. In return, each noble pledged himself to be the king's vassal, or servant, and promised to provide soldiers in time of war.

CASTLE INHABITANTS

INSIDE THE CASTLE, EVERYONE was busy. The lord was about to visit another part of his lands, so there was plenty to get ready. Grooms harnessed the horses and loaded the carts, while squires armed the knights of the lord's escort, and kitchen staff prepared food for the journey. The ladies-in-waiting packed fine clothes for the lord and his family and the chaplain prayed for a safe journey. The lord himself gave final instructions to his constable, who took charge when he was away. Half the garrison went with the lord, so the constable would have to keep a sharp lookout in case the castle was attacked.

THE FAMILY

The castle was not just a stronghold – it was a home for the lord and his family. They were attended by ladies-in-waiting and other servants, who were under the control of the chamberlain.

Lady   Children   Chamberlain
Lady-in-waiting

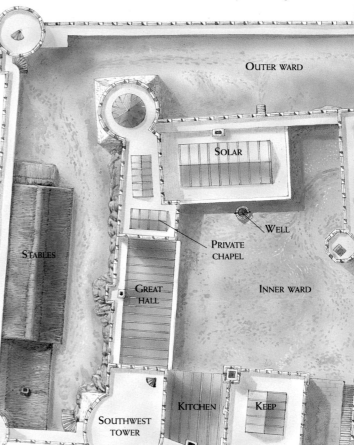

OUTER WARD

SOLAR

WELL

PRIVATE CHAPEL

STABLES

INNER WARD

GREAT HALL

KITCHEN   KEEP

SOUTHWEST TOWER

ARMS AND ARMOUR

Stable grooms looked after the horses belonging to the lord and his knights. In the nearby workshops, the blacksmith made horseshoes and other metal objects, and the armourer mended weapons and armour.

Blacksmith
Armourer   Groom

BUSINESS IN THE HALL

By day, the hall was the centre of castle business. The lord, with his steward and treasurer, collected rents (both cash and crops) and taxes, and punished wrongdoers. At night, minstrels and jesters entertained the dinner guests.

Brewer   Vintner   Butler

BEER AND WINE

Water was not always safe to drink. The brewer made enough beer for everyone each week. The vintner supplied the wine in large casks and the butler, or "bottler", was in charge of the wine cellar. The butler poured the wine into jugs to be served at the tables.

Jester

Steward   Treasurer   Minstrel

Page

Cook   Scullion   Baker   Trencherman   Pantler

COOK AND COMPANY

The cook's scullions helped to prepare the meals. Pages carried dishes into the hall, and trenchermen served the food. The baker made bread every day except Sunday. The pantler kept the dry-food store, or pantry.

Gong farmer   Constable   Men-at-arms   Archer

MEN-AT-ARMS

The garrison included hired soldiers to guard the castle. They practised archery in the outer ward. The constable was the lord's second-in-command. His room was over the gatehouse (the only way into the castle). The gong farmer cleaned out the gong, or pit under the garderobes (toilets).

Huntsman   Falconer   Dog-keeper

HUNTS AND HAWKS

Hunting was the lord's favourite sport and a way of gathering extra food for the larder. Huntsmen and their dogs caught deer and wild boar. The falconer trained hawks to catch rabbits and game birds. Dog-keepers took great care of the hunting dogs.

Private rooms

The lord's private room, or solar, at Goodrich Castle in Hereford, England. A wooden screen shut off the room from the tower beyond. The original level of the floor (about halfway up the pillar) can still be seen.

FACT file

- Some castles had a huge household. In the 1400s, there were over 400 indoor staff at Windsor Castle in England.

- During a siege at Odiham Castle in Hampshire, England, in 1215, the castle was defended by just three knights and ten men-at-arms.

BARBICAN

GATEHOUSE

CHAPEL

LIVING QUARTERS AND WORKSHOPS   ENTRANCE

SOUTHEAST TOWER

Herald   Squire   Knights of the castle

KNIGHTS AND SQUIRES

Knights were skilled fighters who defended the castle along with the ordinary soldiers. Each knight was served by a young squire. Knights and squires spent hours exercising and training with weapons. The herald carried the lord's messages.

THE CHAPLAIN

The chaplain was a priest who led services in the castle's two chapels. The small one next to the solar was used only by the lord and his family. The other much bigger chapel was used by the garrison and servants.

Chaplain

WOOD WORK

Most things in the castle had to be made on site, so the carpenter was a busy man. He and his assistant made everything from siege engines to gates and everyday objects, such as benches and bowls.

Carpenter

WOMEN'S WORK

The spinster spun sheep's wool into thread, which the weaver turned into cloth. Women made or repaired the clothes for everyone who lived in the castle. The laundress washed the clothes (which were very dirty for the castle inhabitants rarely bathed). These were considered very lowly jobs.

Laundress
Spinster

ON THE ROAD

The lord did not live in this castle all year round. He visited his other lands regularly to see that they were being run properly and to collect his rents. Early one summer morning, he set off with his family and servants and an escort of soldiers, known as his retinue.

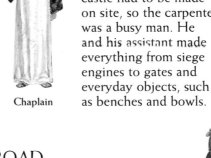

Lord

THE CASTLE'S DEFENCES

WHEN THE LORD RODE AWAY, HE LEFT a stronghold that was as secure as possible. Over the centuries, the castle had been improved to make it difficult to conquer. First, there was a deep ditch. Then an enemy had to break through the outer wall. Beyond this rose another, much higher, wall, bare but for arrow loops. There was only one main entrance through this wall and into the inner part of the castle – the massive gatehouse. This could be blocked with the drawbridge, portcullises, and gates. Surely no one could get through all of that?

ATTACKER BLOCKED
An attacker coming up the stairs would find his right (sword) arm obstructed by the central pillar.

HOME ADVANTAGE
The spiral stairs in each tower rose clockwise. A defender facing downwards had plenty of room to swing his weapon. He could wield his axe in his right hand while he advanced on his attacker.

Well watered
Without a supply of water, the castle could not have lasted through a long siege. It was vital, not just for drinking, but also for putting out fires. The water was drawn up in a bucket from a well over 30 m (98 ft) deep in the corner of the inner ward, near the solar.

LOOK OUT!
The tall tower allowed a clear view over the surrounding countryside and was used as a lookout.

Supplies of fuel, food, and weapons were stored in the old keep.

BOUNCING ROCKS
The swellings at the base of the tower guarded against attack and caused rocks dropped from above to bounce outwards.

STRONG WALLS
The castle walls were over 2 m (6.5 ft) thick at the base.

IN THE DARK
The castle prison was a damp, narrow cell under the keep. There was no light, except when the jailer slid back the bars and opened the thick wooden door. The lord sometimes used the cell to confine noblemen he had captured in battle, rather than common criminals. The noblemen were well fed and not mistreated. They would be set free only when someone had paid their ransom (the money for their release).

MIND THE MOAT
The moat at the base of the castle walls could be either a dry ditch or a wet one. This castle had a dry ditch.

CRENELLATION
Bowmen sheltered behind the upright merlons and shot their arrows through gaps called crenels.

DANGER OVERHEAD

The parapet above the gateway had a slight overhang. It had holes through which defenders could drop stones, boiling oil, or hot sand on soldiers below. This feature was called machicolation.

Murder holes
Anyone entering the gatehouse had to pass beneath "murder holes" in the ceiling above. Defenders could drop missiles or shoot arrows down through these holes. Or, if the attackers set fire to the gates, water could be poured through them.

> "They had warily provided on the walls an abundance of pots full of combustible powders of sulphur and quicklime to cast into the eyes of our men."
>
> Chronicler of the siege of Harfleur, 1415

Guards wound a windlass to raise or lower the portcullis.

Murder holes

The sharpened ends of the portcullis would crush anyone under them.

The enemy could get trapped between the two portcullises.

Arrow loops

THE ONLY OPENINGS in the walls were arrow loops, too narrow for a person to climb through.

Taking cover
A loop was splayed inside so that a bowman could stand comfortably to shoot and not expose himself. From outside it was difficult to shoot through the loops. There were different styles of loops – cross slits made it easier to use a crossbow.

Strong chains raised and lowered the drawbridge.

ENEMY APPROACHING
The drawbridge was made of thick wood and could be hauled up at the appearance of the enemy.

SECURE THE GATE

Four barriers blocked the gateway to attackers. The first was the drawbridge over the ditch, which was raised up to cover the entrance. Next were two portcullises, which were lowered along grooves in the walls. Finally, the heavy gates themselves were shut and barred from the inside.

| Single slit | Cross slit | Cross slit with gun loop |

The Enemy Approaches

TROUBLE WAS NOT LONG in coming. Three days after the lord had left, a rider arrived at the gatehouse with urgent news. The lord's neighbour, a powerful baron, was heading for the castle with a strong army and siege weapons.

A lookout blows a trumpet to warn of strangers approaching.

Mercenary knights arrive to join the garrison of a castle.

The advance of the enemy soldiers is made difficult by the sloping ground in front of the castle.

The outer wall of the castle allowed defenders to shoot at anyone near the walls.

A 15th-century Italian painting of troops besieging a fortress

THE BLACKSMITH

THE CLANG OF THE BLACKSMITH'S hammer and the roar of his forge filled the air. Suddenly, the lookout raced in. "The enemy is near!" he shouted. "The constable says you must make sure all warhorses are well shod and ready for battle!" The blacksmith threw down his heavy hammer. There was no time to lose. Without good shoes, horses were useless, and, without horses, the castle knights could not ride out against the attackers. While the smith's assistant heated up the forge with the bellows, the stable grooms led the horses to the workshop. Then the blacksmith started work. He took off the worn old shoes, fitted new ones, and nailed them on firmly.

AN EARLY WARNING
The lookout ran in to tell the blacksmith that he had seen an enemy army approaching. He knew that the blacksmith needed as much time as possible to shoe the horses.

GREAT HORSE
A knight's horse had to be big and strong, as well as nimble enough to turn quickly in battle.

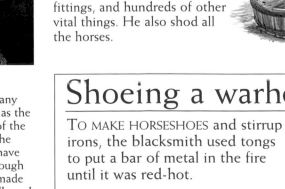

THE ANVIL
The smith hammered the hot metal on his heavy iron anvil, which was fixed to a block of timber set into the floor to keep it steady.

IRON MAN
The blacksmith was a very important craftsman as he made or mended everything metal in the castle. From his dark workshop against the inner wall of the castle, he produced iron nails, chains, tools, locks, gate hinges, parts for giant catapults, wagon fittings, and hundreds of other vital things. He also shod all the horses.

A modern blacksmith
A blacksmith today employs many of the same tools and methods as the medieval blacksmith. The use of the forge, bellows, and anvil, and the techniques for shoeing horses have changed little in 600 years. Though most modern metal goods are made by machines, the blacksmith still needs his skills to shape items such as hand-crafted gates and garden furniture.

Shoeing a warhorse

TO MAKE HORSESHOES and stirrup irons, the blacksmith used tongs to put a bar of metal in the fire until it was red-hot.

Hammering it out
On the anvil, he hammered the iron into shape. He made buckles for the stirrup straps and punched holes in the horseshoes for the nails.

Stirrup iron   Horseshoe

FITTING THE SHOE
The smith's assistant picked up each foot of the warhorse in turn, took off the old shoe, and trimmed away untidy bits of hoof with his rasp. Then he made sure the new shoe fitted and nailed it on.

DOUBLE BLAST
The forge had two sets of bellows. When one was opened to draw in air, the other was closed. This created a constant blast of air into the forge.

BURNING MATTER
The charcoal for the forge was made by cutting down trees from the lord's estates and partly burning the wood in a special outdoor hearth.

The blacksmith and his helpers wore thick leather aprons to protect themselves from flying sparks and burning metal.

Water for cooling and tempering iron

TURNING CARTWHEELS
The carpenter wanted an iron rim, or tyre, fitted onto a new wooden cartwheel. His assistant brought it to the smith, who would heat a bar of iron and beat it out flat, then bend it into a large ring.

A TIGHT FIT
The boy waited for the smith's helper to fit the tyre. He would have to heat the metal tyre again to make it expand and slip easily over the wheel. Then he would pour cold water on it so that it cooled and shrank tight.

FORGING AHEAD
The heart of the blacksmith's shop was the forge, a brick box with a charcoal fire and flue to draw off the smoke and fumes. The forge was big, but the fire itself was small. It was right in the centre of the mass of charcoal, and was kept blazing hot with regular blasts of air from the bellows at the side. The smith's helper worked the bellows by pulling the handle up and down.

Making chain

CHAIN WAS USED to shackle prisoners and lift the drawbridge. It was even bedded into walls to strengthen them.

Chain was also used for carthorse harnesses.

Nippers   Snips

Tools of the trade
A blacksmith's tools included tongs to hold hot pieces of metal, snips to cut thin metal sheets, and nippers to hold and draw wire.

Tongs

Links in the chain
The smith hammered each link into a loop and joined it to the next link in the chain. For heavy-duty chains, he also put a brace across each link to make it stronger.

Cartwheels today
Carpenters called wheelwrights still make and repair the wooden wheels that are used on horsedrawn carts. The outer part of each wheel is made in several sections, called felloes. The spokes are wedged into the felloes, joining them to the wheel hub. Blacksmiths still fit metal tyres to protect the wooden wheels from wear and tear. It is necessary for the tyres to be heated and cooled evenly, so that they grip the wood properly.

THE CASTLE GARRISON

IN TIMES OF PEACE, THE LORD kept only a few soldiers to guard the castle. There were three knights who lived as part of his permanent household, and a handful of men-at-arms. But recently, danger had threatened. For some months, the lord had been expecting an assault from his ambitious and powerful neighbour, the baron. As a precaution, he had hired many more knights and soldiers to fight for him. This was an expensive business. Each knight was paid two shillings (10p) a day, and each mounted man-at-arms, one shilling (5p). With a garrison of over 60 men – each of whom needed food and stabling for his horses – the weekly bills were enormous.

KNIGHTS

The knights were soldiers of high rank who had trained in battle skills since childhood. They were experts in horse riding, wrestling, and fighting with all kinds of weapons, including swords, lances, axes, and maces.

HIRED SOLDIERS

A lord's tenants had to carry out guard duty at the castle as part of their rent. This service was unpopular by the 14th century, and many of the tenants paid this rent in cash. The lord used this money to hire bands of mercenaries, or professional soldiers.

MOUNTED MEN-AT-ARMS

The men-at-arms were lower in rank than the knights, but they also fought on horseback. Armour was expensive, so ordinary cavalrymen often wore only a few pieces of plate armour over a coat of mail.

A mail curtain covered the neck.

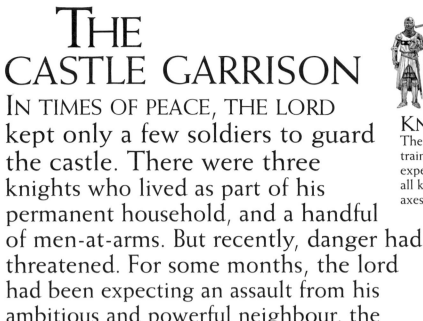

ARMOUR-PLATED

Arrows from longbows or quarrels from crossbows could pierce mail. So a knight covered his arms, legs, and body with specially shaped steel plates. Steel gauntlets (armoured gloves) covered his hands, and a steel basinet (helmet) protected his head.

A knight's shield was made of wood. It was smaller than in earlier centuries and slightly curved to give greater protection to the soldier's body.

FOOT SOLDIERS

The infantry wore coats of mail and quilted canvas tunics (collarless jackets) for protection. On their heads, they wore helmets of leather or metal. They fought with swords and bucklers (small fist shields) or with spears or axes.

BOWMEN

Archers with longbows or crossbows could shoot accurately over a long distance. They were vital for picking off attackers.

A squire practises acrobatics.

In this late 19th-century romantic painting, a lady dubs, or knights, a squire.

TOUGH TRAINING

A knight's apprenticeship (training period) was long and hard. At about the age of seven, he was sent to serve as a page in a nobleman's household. Here, he would learn good manners, singing, and how to play music. At 14, he became a squire, serving a knight. His training began with wrestling, sword fighting, and the art of riding and caring for his horse.

WATCH YOUR WEIGHT

The quintain was a training device. It was a cutout figure with a shield on one side and a weight on the other. The squire rode towards it, trying to hit the shield with his lance. This caused the quintain to spin. The squire had to be quick to avoid the weight as it swung round!

BECOMING A KNIGHT

When he was about 21, the squire became a knight. At a special ceremony, he was dressed in new clothes and given a sword and spurs. He knelt before his master or the king, who touched his neck with a sword. The new knight vowed to fight for good, to protect the poor, and to pursue evildoers.

GLAIVE
This single-edged blade on a long staff, called a glaive, could be used for both stabbing and slashing.

BOW ATTACK
The longbow was usually made of wood from the yew tree. It was about as tall as the archer himself.

WEAPONS OF WAR

A knight on horseback had a wide choice of weapons. First, he charged at his enemy with a long lance. Then he drew his pointed thrusting sword, specially made to jab into gaps between armour plates. He could also attack his enemy with a short mace. A soldier fighting on foot could get a more powerful swing with longer weapons, such as an axe, which had a handle nearly 2 m (6 ft 5 in) long, and which could split a skull down to the teeth.

A war sword from the 14th century

SWORD
The blade of a thrusting sword was made stronger by a thick centre that tapered towards the edges.

MACE
A strike from this studded ball mounted on a short haft could dent even armour plates.

AXE
The short-handled axe with its vicious spike was easy to swing on horseback.

LONGBOW
A longbowman bent the bow away from him with his left hand and pulled the string with his right hand before letting go.

A mace from the 14th century (with a modern haft)

A 14th-century short axe

PREPARING FOR THE BATTLE

NEWS OF THE BARON'S ADVANCE spread swiftly through the surrounding countryside. In panic, people from nearby villages and hamlets abandoned their homes and hurried towards the shelter of the town. Meanwhile, the castle constable put his garrison on full alert. He sent messengers out to summon extra soldiers. He ordered supplies of food, water, and ammunition to be brought into the town and stored. He arranged for the carpenter to strengthen the castle defences by building wooden hoardings on the tops of the walls and towers. And he dispatched a rider with a message for the lord, begging him for advice on the best course of action.

> "There was within the town neither maid or woman, who did not carry a stone to the palisade to cast."
>
> Chronicler of the siege of Dunwich 1173-4

CASTLE STORE
Stores of weapons and provisions were carried up to the castle.

A mercenary carried his bedding and some food.

A peasant may have walked all day to reach the castle.

Mounted men-at-arms rode their horses.

HEADING FOR SAFETY

On the road to the town, there was a steady stream of ox carts, donkeys, and people on foot. The villagers carried with them everything they owned – iron pots and tools, woollen blankets, and rough furniture. Most valuable of all were the animals. Everyone had a few chickens, and richer peasants had cows and a couple of sheep.

VALUABLE ANIMALS
The peasants brought their animals into the town. They made sure that nothing was left behind for the attackers to eat.

Generally, horses were too valuable, and often too weak, to haul the bulky wooden carts on rutted roads. Oxen were used instead.

A carpenter puts up a side screen to keep out arrows.

Slats were laid with gaps left between them for missiles to be dropped through.

Supporting beams were placed in special "putlog" holes in the masonry of the wall.

Hot sand or oil could be poured, or stones pushed, through the gaps in the base of the hoarding.

Lookouts stood on each castle tower.

BOARDING UP
The castle carpenter hastily erected a timber gallery, or hoarding, around the tops of the towers and along the curtain walls. This protected defenders from arrows, and allowed them to drop missiles onto attackers below.

Castle livestock
DURING A LONG SIEGE, fresh food was vital. Farm animals kept inside the castle provided meat and milk.

Chickens   Pig

Animals for food
Cows, goats, and sheep were milked every day. Hens gave eggs and meat. Pigs were killed and their meat was preserved by salting or smoking.

BOLTED AND BARRED
The constable's first aim was to prevent the attackers reaching the castle wall. His men cleared the hillside of rocks and bushes so that there was nothing to hide behind. He stationed archers in the barbican in front of the gatehouse. Then the portcullises were dropped, the drawbridge wound up, and the inner gates bolted and jammed from behind with baulks of timber.

SCORCHED EARTH
The constable ordered villagers to destroy their houses and fields of standing crops. Any grain that could not be stored in the town or castle was burned, and surplus livestock slaughtered and buried. This prevented the enemy getting their hands on it: their army was large and needed plenty of food.

BURN IT DOWN
The flimsy peasant huts, made of timber, mud, and straw or reed thatching, burned very easily.

The peasant's carefully tended barley went up in flames to deprive the enemy of food.

Mercenary carrying his own sword, lance, and buckler (small shield).

A cartload of stones to throw from the walls.

After burning, the ground was left scorched and bare.

REINFORCEMENTS
Once, castle lords had relied on the tenants of their lands to do guard duty as a way of paying rent. But now, most tenants paid cash. When the castle needed extra troops, bands of mercenaries were hired. These were skilled professionals who brought their own weapons with them.

THE FIRST ATTACK

THE ATTACKING army had a long march. It wasn't so bad for the knights on horseback, but the unfortunate foot soldiers had to walk all the way. First they needed to capture the town, and then they could take the castle. The troops pitched their tents, set up their siege machines, and went to work. The archers set alight the thatched roofs with flaming arrows. Foot soldiers battered down the main gates with a ram, while others scrambled up ladders and over the walls. Most people in the town fled. Those who were left surrendered – the town had fallen.

A MEAN MACHINE

Before long, the trebuchet (giant catapult) had smashed great holes in the town walls. On one end of a huge wooden beam was a heavy weight and on the other, a sling. Operators were busy pulling the arm down, loading the sling with stones, then letting it go.

SLINGSHOT
The sling was designed to open in midair, releasing the missile inside.

MISSILE LAUNCH
When released, the arm of the trebuchet flew up in the air, launching its contents into the sky.

SETTING UP CAMP
One of the first tasks of the attacking army was to make camp.

COUNTER BALANCE
A counterweight filled with rocks and soil helped the pivoting arm of the trebuchet to swing over.

AMMUNITION
The usual ammunition for the trebuchet was large stone balls weighing about 45–90 kg (100–200 lbs).

Behind strong walls

This painting shows the thick stone walls surrounding a medieval town in France. The walls protected the inhabitants from enemies. Strong gates were the only entrances and all these were locked at dusk and not opened again until dawn.

HITTING THE TARGET

Bull's-eye! Lumps of rock flew everywhere as the missile knocked a chunk from the town's walls and shattered into pieces. Soldiers tumbled back from the parapet, and a huge cheer went up from the attacking army.

Incendiary (flaming) arrows set the roof alight, and the fire spread quickly.

DANGEROUS FRAGMENTS
Sometimes the missile would break up into tiny fragments. The fragments could fly off like bullets and cause terrible wounds.

FIRE!
Fire destroyed the dry, wooden shingles on the roof.

DEFENSIVE MEASURES
Defending soldiers used "murder holes" to spy through or to drop objects onto the attacking army below.

The portcullis fitted into grooves in the walls and so could not be forced inwards

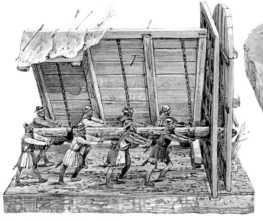

BREAKING IN

The attackers broke down the town gate with a battering ram. The ram was slung by chains from a wooden shelter. Its roof was covered with raw, damp animal hides to protect the attacking soldiers from incendiary missiles thrown down at them from the town walls.

GETTING INSIDE
Once through the gate, the attacking army could set fire to the wooden houses inside the town.

THROUGH THE GATEWAY

The gatehouse was often the only way into a walled town. In times of danger, the gate would be bolted and jammed shut with strong wooden bars.

LONG WEEKS OF SIEGE

IT WAS STALEMATE. THE ATTACKERS COULD not take the castle by a direct assault, and the defenders could not drive them. away. The baron seethed with anger and frustration. He had stripped the town and nearby countryside of food for his army. There was only one way left – to starve the garrison into surrender. The baron set guards around the castle to stop any reinforcements or fresh supplies getting in. Then he waited. Days turned into weeks; weeks became a whole month. The stores of food, fuel, and arrows inside the walls of the castle began to run perilously low.

> ### EYEWITNESS
> "Shoot not your arrows, except in great need. If we have food, let us save it willingly. Spare your weapons, I say to you archers."
>
> Roger d'Estuteville at Wark-on-Tweed, 1174

BEHIND THE BATTLEMENTS
In spite of the protection of the merlons, a soldier was hit by an enemy arrow. The wounded man was helped downstairs to the surgeon.

SICK BAY
Injured people were tended on the first floor of the keep. They lay on the straw while the surgeon removed arrowheads and bound up wounds.

THE STORE
Food (including corn, salted pork, and dried beans) and firewood was stored in the basement. This was kept locked to stop pilfering (stealing).

Herbal medicine

Plant cures
Many different herbs grew in the little castle garden. They had two major uses – to mask the taste of rotten meat and to make medicines. Dill helped the digesting of food and was also believed to ward off witches' spells. Mint could cure over 40 illnesses, from bad memory to headaches. Hyssop was famous as a laxative, and the scent of fennel revived anyone feeling faint.

Dill   Mint   Hyssop   Fennel

AFTER TWO WEEKS
For a time, there were no more attempts to storm the castle. But the guards kept watch and tried to pick off enemy soldiers with their crossbows. The baron's men shot back and flung another missile from their trebuchets. Some of the garrison sheltered in the keep. This is where they would make their last stand if the enemy overran the walls.

AFTER FOUR WEEKS

Day after day, the summer sun beat down. In the fierce heat, stored water and meat quickly bred germs. Dysentery (an infection that causes diarrhoea) spread among the half-starved castle dwellers. Soon disease was killing more people than the enemy, and morale among the soldiers was very low.

KEEPING WATCH
The lookout pointed to the horizon. There was a large army heading towards the castle. Above it, he could see the lord's banner fluttering in the breeze. They were saved!

RELIEF AT LAST
More than half the garrison was dead, and the well was dry. Some survivors begged the constable to surrender the castle. They could scarcely hold out against another assault. The message from the eastern tower came just in time.

The chaplain gave his blessing to a dying man and anointed him with oil.

LOSING HOPE
Exhausted and ill-fed, the defenders on the parapet began to despair.

DIRECT HIT
A missile from a trebuchet tore a jagged hole in the timber of the keep.

RUNNING LOW
Soldiers opened the last two barrels of arrows for ammunition for their longbows.

The physician gave herbal medicines to those struck down with dysentery.

SEARING FLESH
The surgeon cauterized a wound with a red-hot iron to burn off infected flesh and to stop bleeding.

Barrels were torn apart for fuel.

EMPTY STORE
The last scraps of food had been eaten.

BARON FLEES
Even as the lord's army approached, men were dying inside the castle. Outside, the besiegers were also suffering from lack of food as well as sickness. At the sight of the lord's soldiers returning, the attackers fled.

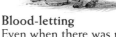

Blood-letting
Even when there was no food, people were reluctant to kill their livestock, especially horses or other pack animals, such as donkeys. Instead, they drained off a small amount of the animal's blood and drank it.

AFTER SIX WEEKS
The defenders were so hungry that they searched for anything that might be edible. They hunted for rats and mice to cook and munched grass and dry thistles. Then they cut the leather hide from the horses' saddles, boiled it until it was soft, and chewed the pieces.

Peace Returns

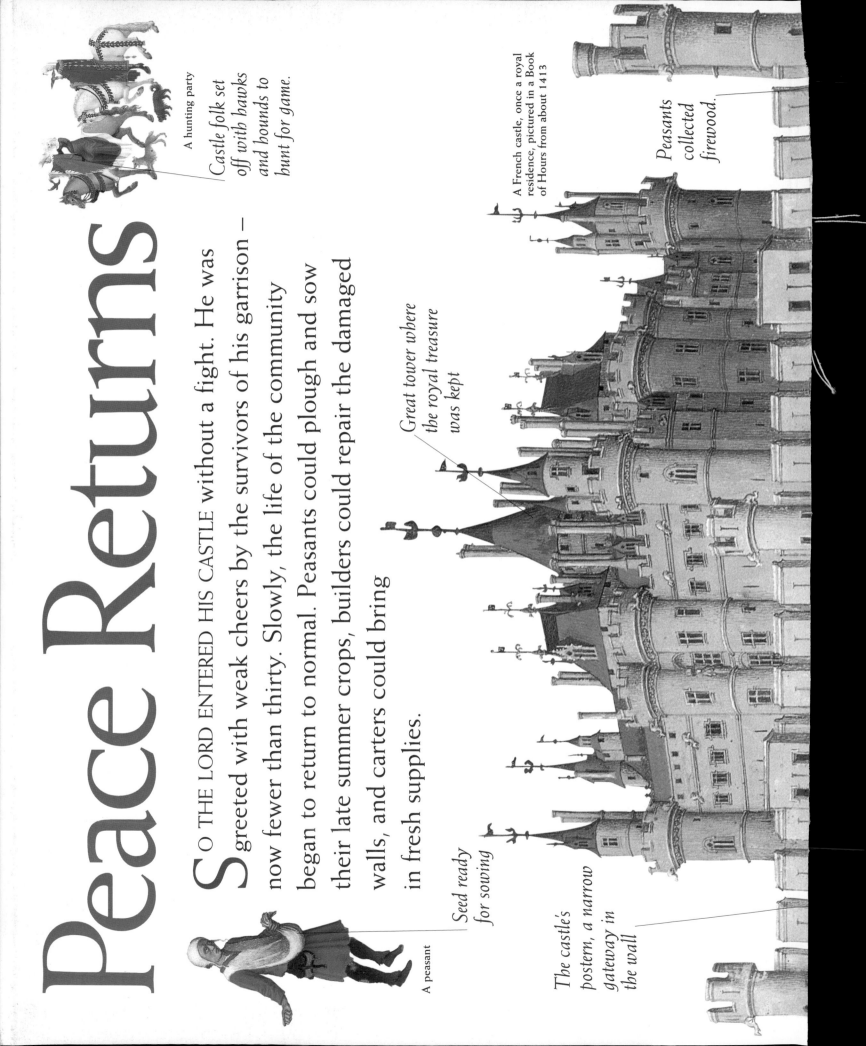

S O THE LORD ENTERED HIS CASTLE without a fight. He was greeted with weak cheers by the survivors of his garrison – now fewer than thirty. Slowly, the life of the community began to return to normal. Peasants could plough and sow their late summer crops, builders could repair the damaged walls, and carters could bring in fresh supplies.

A hunting party

Castle folk set off with hawks and hounds to hunt for game.

A French castle, once a royal residence, pictured in a Book of Hours from about 1413

Peasants collected firewood.

Great tower where the royal treasure was kept

A peasant

Seed ready for sowing

The castle's postern, a narrow gateway in the wall

THE CASTLE LANDS

THE COUNTRYSIDE AROUND THE CASTLE was in a sorry state. Fields and hedges had been trampled and trees cut down for firewood by the invading army. But it was still summer, and there would be time for any crops the villagers planted to ripen before harvest time. This was vital. If they did not grow enough food now, they might starve during the winter. The arable land around each village was divided into three areas. The areas were used in rotation, so that one lay fallow, and the others were ploughed and planted. The villagers had strips of land in each of the areas. Now they ploughed their strips as swiftly as possible and sowed barley, oats, wheat, and vegetables.

Caring for the vines
Farm work never stopped, except during the rains and frosts of midwinter. In late winter, villagers pruned their grapevines and other fruit bushes by cutting away the dead and diseased wood.

Sowing the seeds
In early spring, peasants sowed grain seed on their strips of land. The sower took handfuls of seed from the bag around his neck and broadcast (scattered) it over the soil as evenly as he could.

Crushing the grapes
Ripe grapes were harvested and processed into wine in early autumn. A peasant squashed his or her grapes underfoot. The juice was collected and left to ferment.

HONEY HARVEST
Bees buzz angrily as this woman prepares to take honeycomb from one of her hives in late summer. Honey was a very popular ingredient in cooking in the 14th century. It was needed for sweetening and preserving food. Sugar was still an expensive – and very rare – luxury.

Animals on the land

IN LATE AUTUMN, many animals were slaughtered as there would not be enough for them to eat during the winter. Their meat was preserved.

Cotswold sheep
Sheep's wool was a valuable crop. The sheep were shorn in midsummer and the fleeces sold to be woven into cloth. Mutton was a popular meat.

Bagot goat
Goats were tethered on waste ground to browse on rough grass and scrub. They provided milk and meat, as well as hair for weaving.

FACT file

- Peasants were required to pay tithes to the village priest. These consisted of a tenth of their produce.
- Most villagers were serfs. This meant that they were not allowed to leave the lord's lands without his permission.
- Peasants had to get their corn ground at the lord's mill. The lord kept a part of their crop as payment.
- The lord's tenants (peasants living in villages on the lord's land) had to sow, plough, and harvest the lord's crops.

Grain of wheat still in its husk

A reeve carried a white stick as a mark of his position.

HAY HARVEST
In midsummer, grass was cut with scythes to make hay. Once turned and dried in the sun, it was picked up with pitchforks and built into stacks with thatched tops to keep off the rain.

A pitchfork was used for gathering hay bundles and tossing them into a wagon.

"Beak"

Sickle
During the summer months, an iron sickle was used for cutting crops.

Billhook
This tool had a long cutting edge and a handy "beak".

VILLAGE OFFICER
The reeve was elected by other villagers to oversee their work. He made sure that everyone performed their duties for the lord, especially at harvest time (as shown in the picture above) when there was a great deal of work to do. In return, he was paid a fee and sometimes ate at the lord's table.

FARMING CROPS
Grain crops (such as wheat or barley) were cut down with sickles and bunched into sheaves, before being threshed to separate the grain from the husks. Cattle fed on the stubble left in the fields.

USEFUL TOOL
The billhook was one of the peasant's most versatile tools. He used it to trim hedges, prune fruit trees, and split firewood for kindling. The billhook was even adapted for use on the battlefield.

Huge, curving white horns

Longhorn cow
A cow was used in three ways: to give milk, to provide meat, and to pull ploughs and carts. Its hide was tanned to make leather, and its horns were made into spoons, cups, and even window coverings.

Milk from the cow was preserved as butter or cheese.

PANNAGE
Peasants knocked acorns out of oak trees for their pigs to eat. As other food became scarce in autumn, acorns and beechnuts were good for fattening pigs. The lord gave the right to do this (called pannage) to his serfs.

THE HUNTING PARTY

THE GATE OF THE DEER PARK swung open. The hunters on horseback, jumped over the ditch and into the park. Startled by the huntsmen the fallow deer ran in all directions. The blast of hunting horn and the yelps of hounds filled the air. Wide-eyed in fear, the deer bounded away. After them came the hounds and the stream of nobles on horseback, led by the lord. A long way behind, panting and red-faced, trailed the servants and villagers on foot. A deer hunt thrilled everyone. In times of peace, the chase gave the knights a chance to practise their riding skills. Hunting was part of the education of every young nobleman.

> "...If the boar be stronger than you then you must turn from side to side as best you can without letting go the haft until God comes to your aid..."
>
> Gaston Phoebus from
> *Le Livre de la Chasse,*
> late 14th century

FEARSOME
A wild boar was a dangerous animal, as heavy as two men. Boar hunters carried special spears that had razor-sharp points. A crosspiece could be fitted to the spear to stop the boar rushing right up the weapon.

RELEASE THE DOGS
The hunting dogs included alaunts (like mastiffs), who grappled with the boar.

LOOK OUT!
Villagers' land was often trampled by the horses.

The dogs wore coats to protect them from the fierce tusks of the boar.

Dog boys
The lord took great care of his hounds. He employed kennel boys to feed the dogs, give them medicine if they were sick, pull out thorns from their paws, patch up their wounds after a hunt, and take them for runs in the meadows. The boys would even sleep in the straw with the dogs.

BEWARE OF THE BOAR
The dogs held the boar until the huntsman came to kill it. When the boar charged, the hunter held one end of the boar spear tucked under his arm and against the ground to take the shock, and kept the point facing the animal.

TERRIBLE TUSKS
One slash from a boar's tusks could cause dreadful wounds.

SIGHTING PREY
When the falconer spotted suitable prey, he removed the bird's hood and allowed the falcon to fly.

Women usually flew smaller birds, such as merlins.

Powerful birds were reserved for the lord to fly.

Falconry

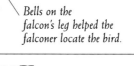

THE FALCON WORE A HOOD so that it couldn't see its surroundings. This kept it calm.

Protective leather glove

Care of the bird
The lord even carried his peregrine when he was doing business in the great hall. To make sure that the bird didn't fly away, it was tied to the lord's finger with a long silk string. This was called a jess.

Peregrine falcon

Bells on the falcon's leg helped the falconer locate the bird.

BIRD IN HAND
The lord's favourite sport was falconry. He carried his falcon on his right wrist, which was protected from the bird's fierce talons by a thick leather glove. At his command, the bird flew off to catch wildfowl, such as duck.

BEATING THE BUSHES
Trackers lay in wait in the undergrowth. They scared the deer into the glade, where the huntsmen could attack.

Hound's reward
After the deer was caught and killed came the "unmaking", or cleaning. The huntsman slit open the deer's belly and fed its insides to the hounds as a reward. Then the huntsmen slung the deer on a pole and carried it back to the castle.

DEER HUNT
Today the lord and his huntsmen were chasing a deer – this was the best game in the forest. The huntsman controlled his hounds by shouts or by calls on his horn. If the hunters came across a wolf they would track it and kill it because wolves killed their sheep.

THE LORD'S FOREST
The lord carefully guarded his right to hunt in the forests. Anyone else caught hunting (poaching) would be punished severely, possibly even hanged.

DEER FOR THE TABLE
After the deer was caught and killed, it would be eaten by the lord and his family.

Hunting crossbow

HUNTING WITH A CROSSBOW allowed men and women to practise their archery skills. Small crossbows, often decorated, were used to shoot hares or wildfowl.

Hunting crossbow 1450–1470

Bowstring of twisted cord

Shooting arrows
A hunter could use a crossbow on horseback. It was very accurate and shot short arrows called bolts.

Blunt head for knocking down game

TAKE AIM
When the trigger underneath was pulled, this revolving nut was released.

Barbed triangular head

Reloading
The trouble with a crossbow was that it took a long time to reload. The hunter had to wind back the string and slip it over a nut.

THE GREAT FEAST

ALL MORNING, DELICIOUS COOKING smells had drifted from the castle kitchens. Servants had prepared the great hall for the celebration feast, putting up long trestle tables and setting out knives, wooden bowls, spoons, and cups. On the high table, where the lord would sit, the spoons and cups were silver. When all was ready, a horn summoned the diners. They quickly filled the benches – the most important people sat at the end nearest the high table. After a blessing, a procession of servants carried in the steaming dishes. The sound of chattering and laughter filled the hall as the feasting began.

ROAST MEAT
A scullion turned the roasting boar on a spit in front of the fire to make sure that it cooked evenly.

THE KITCHEN

Meat was either roasted on a spit or stewed in a huge iron pot over the fire. The kitchen also contained an oven for baking bread. Scullions prepared the food at the central table.

TRENCHERS
Meat dishes were usually served on slabs of stale bread, called trenchers, instead of plates. The bread soaked up the gravy and afterwards it might be given to the poor to eat.

TABLE MANNERS

Good table manners were encouraged. Diners often shared dishes, so they had to wipe their fingers and spoons regularly. They should not belch, stuff their mouths, put their elbows on the table, or dip meat in the salt dish.

Wine cups
needed frequent refilling.

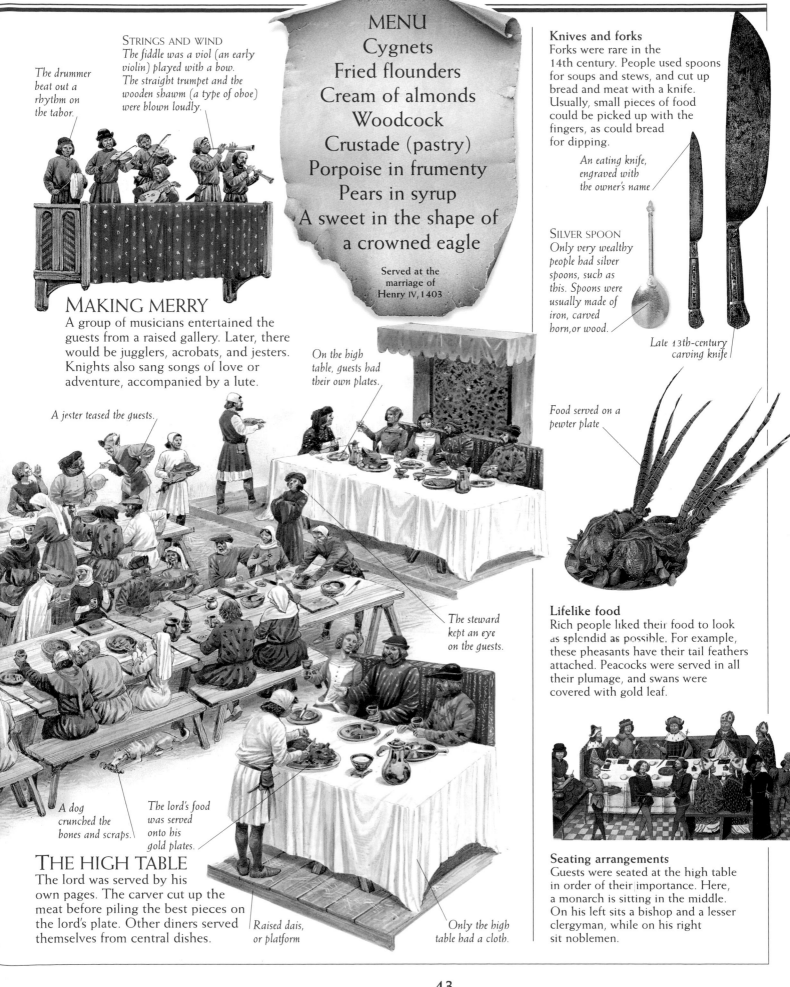

STRINGS AND WIND
The fiddle was a viol (an early violin) played with a bow. The straight trumpet and the wooden shawm (a type of oboe) were blown loudly.

The drummer beat out a rhythm on the tabor.

MENU
Cygnets
Fried flounders
Cream of almonds
Woodcock
Crustade (pastry)
Porpoise in frumenty
Pears in syrup
A sweet in the shape of
a crowned eagle

Served at the marriage of Henry IV, 1403

Knives and forks
Forks were rare in the 14th century. People used spoons for soups and stews, and cut up bread and meat with a knife. Usually, small pieces of food could be picked up with the fingers, as could bread for dipping.

An eating knife, engraved with the owner's name

SILVER SPOON
Only very wealthy people had silver spoons, such as this. Spoons were usually made of iron, carved horn, or wood.

Late 13th-century carving knife

MAKING MERRY
A group of musicians entertained the guests from a raised gallery. Later, there would be jugglers, acrobats, and jesters. Knights also sang songs of love or adventure, accompanied by a lute.

A jester teased the guests.

On the high table, guests had their own plates.

The steward kept an eye on the guests.

Food served on a pewter plate

Lifelike food
Rich people liked their food to look as splendid as possible. For example, these pheasants have their tail feathers attached. Peacocks were served in all their plumage, and swans were covered with gold leaf.

A dog crunched the bones and scraps.

The lord's food was served onto his gold plates.

THE HIGH TABLE
The lord was served by his own pages. The carver cut up the meat before piling the best pieces on the lord's plate. Other diners served themselves from central dishes.

Raised dais, or platform

Only the high table had a cloth.

Seating arrangements
Guests were seated at the high table in order of their importance. Here, a monarch is sitting in the middle. On his left sits a bishop and a lesser clergyman, while on his right sit noblemen.

REAL-LIFE SIEGES

S IEGES WERE AT THE HEART of warfare from Roman times until the late Middle Ages. Even after that, castles and cities sometimes tried to sit out an attack. The two sides in the conflict were often evenly matched – defenders safe behind strong walls, and attackers relying on a blockade or an assault with siege machines. But the development of modern firearms eventually led to the end of the castle's impregnability. Cannonballs and shells could destroy even the thickest walls, and rockets and bombers could fly over them.

1099 JERUSALEM
After Antioch, the crusaders moved on in blazing heat to the Holy City of Jerusalem. Smouldering sacks produced a smoke screen, and attackers stormed over the walls from belfry towers.

1189–92 ACRE
Acre (now Akko in Israel) stood on a triangle of land jutting out into the sea. The crusaders attacked with stones from a giant catapult named "Evil Neighbour" and by undermining the walls. Finally, the citizens surrendered.

1429 ORLEANS
The invading English army had built a ring of forts around the French town of Orleans. Mounted on a white charger, 17-year-old Joan of Arc led a series of French counterattacks, captured the forts, and relieved the siege.

The entrance to the Golden Horn seaway was blocked.

The Sultan's army camped outside the city walls. It was 20 times bigger than the defending force.

1453 CONSTANTINOPLE
Constantinople had been a Christian city for 1,000 years. Then the Turkish sultan dragged his warships overland into the Golden Horn and attacked from the sea. Meanwhile, his artillery fired from the land. Turkish troops invaded, and the city was reborn as the Islamic Istanbul.

Strong castle walls protected Rhodes.

The Turkish leaders discuss their tactics, while overlooking the city.

1097–8 ANTIOCH
It took Christian crusader armies eight months to overcome the Muslim defenders of Antioch (now Antakya, Turkey). There were mountains on one side of the city and marshes on another. The crusaders hurled around 200 Turkish heads into the city. Eventually, a treacherous armourer let in the besiegers, and following desperate fighting, Antioch fell.

1480 RHODES
Rhodes was a well-defended Mediterranean island held by an order of Christian knights. When a huge Turkish army landed, soldiers bombarded the walls with guns and engines. In spite of many attacks, the Turks failed to get into the city and fled, leaving hundreds of dead. But Rhodes did eventually fall in 1522, ending Christian power in the eastern Mediterranean.

1565 MALTA

Ousted from Rhodes, the Christian knights went to Malta. However, another massive Turkish fleet arrived, attacking their fort, St. Elmo. The tiny garrison held out for three months before being overwhelmed. This allowed enough time for a relieving army to arrive, and the Turks then withdrew.

1615 OSAKA

The Japanese warlord Ieyasu besieged Osaka, the stronghold of his rival, Hideyori. Unable to take it by force, he persuaded the defenders that he would leave peacefully only if his soldiers were allowed to fill in the outer moat around Osaka. Hideyori reluctantly agreed. Later, Ieyasu returned with an army of 250,000 men. He defeated the warriors of Osaka, entered the castle, and destroyed it by fire.

Enemy fire destroyed the fort's northern wall, killing many of the defenders.

Out of the range of enemy guns, workers dug their way under Chitor's stone walls.

1567 CHITOR

When the ruler of Chitor in India refused to recognize Akbar, the Moghul ruler, as his overlord, Akbar attacked Chitor's enormous fort. It was thought that the fort's stone walls were impregnable, but Akbar's army attacked with cannons, while digging three mines under the walls. Eventually, the defenders of Chitor opened the city gates to take on their attackers face-to-face. After fierce fighting, Chitor fell.

1854 SEBASTOPOL

Sebastopol, the main Russian naval base, was besieged for 12 months by British and French troops. Disease, confusion, and a harsh winter hampered the attackers, but finally, the Russians blew up their ammunition and marched away.

1864 ATLANTA

At the height of the American Civil War, General Sherman's Union army advanced on Atlanta. They cut off all supplies to the city and shelled rebel lines. After a month, the starving and exhausted defenders fled, leaving the city ablaze.

THE SIEGE OF ATLANTA, 1864

Earthworks provided a better vantage point.

1870 PARIS

Prussian invaders (from what is now Germany and northern Europe) stopped food supplies and fired over 400 shells a day into Paris. Hungry citizens were forced to eat rats, cats, and dogs. Early in 1871, the city fell, and the Prussians marched in triumph through the city streets.

HOW CASTLES WERE BUILT

EARLY CASTLES, MADE OF timber and earthwork, were quick and cheap to build. Some were raised in only eight days! But a massive stone castle took many years to complete and was very expensive. In 1198, Chateau Gaillard, built in France by Richard I, cost more than £11,000. At that time, a castle chaplain earned about £1.50 a year and a knight, £20. Stone, iron, and other materials often had to be brought from far away, and a huge workforce (sometimes as great as 3,000 men) was needed.

BUILDING WALLS

Stone was either cut from nearby quarries or transported to the site by boat or cart. The stone in some English castles was brought all the way from France.

Groundwork

Wherever possible, a castle was built on solid rock foundations. In soft ground, workers dug trenches, filled them with rammed rubble, and built the walls on top.

Extracting stone

Quarry workers cut stone from the ground by hammering iron wedges into the layers of rock. The stone split into massive rough blocks that could be lifted out.

Workers used a pulley system to raise stones.

A barrow of stones could be hauled up a ramp with ropes.

Labourers carried baskets of mortar up ladders.

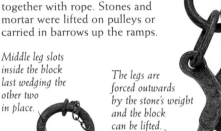

MEDIEVAL METHODS OF LIFTING STONE

Scaffolding

As the wall grew higher, the masons erected wooden scaffolding lashed together with rope. Stones and mortar were lifted on pulleys or carried in barrows up the ramps.

Middle leg slots inside the block last wedging the other two in place.

The legs are forced outwards by the stone's weight and the block can be lifted.

TWO-LEGGED LEWIS

CROSS-SECTION OF SMALL LEWIS

Lifting tackle

The heavy blocks were raised with lewises, whose legs fitted into a tapered slot cut into the top of the stone.

Master and men

A master mason, highly skilled in stone construction, was in charge of all the building operations. He surveyed the site, drew up plans, and ordered materials. He also hired the men, such as the stone mason and woodworker shown above, and gave them precise instructions.

Begun in about 1271, Caerphilly was the work of Gilbert de Clare. It is a huge castle with defences including round towers, heavily defended gatehouses, and two lines of walls.

The right site

Castles were usually built at strategically important spots, such as a commanding hill top with a good view over the countryside, or near a river crossing. Many builders adapted the natural terrain to make the castle easier to defend. Caerphilly Castle, Wales, shown here, was surrounded by a wide moat, formed by diverting water from a nearby lake.

Layer masons built the walls.

Mixing mortar

The stones were bound together with mortar, made by mixing sand, lime, and water. Other ingredients might include chopped horsehair, straw, wood ash, ox blood, or even eggs!

Building tools

STONE MASONS had to master a huge variety of techniques. Apart from walls, they had to build spiral staircases (the pieces of which slotted over one another exactly), machicolations, rounded towers, and arrow loops. The lord might also require decorative work inside the castle chambers, such as carved fireplaces and fan vaulting for the ceiling of the chapel.

Curved end for prising out and shifting heavy blocks

Working with stone
Masons used many different tools, each with its own special purpose. There were different chisels for splitting stone, smoothing the face of a block, and carving outlines or decorative designs. They also used trammels for scoring guide marks, iron hammers, and wooden mallets.

Wing for holding the measuring arm in place

Measuring out
Blocks of stone, especially curved or intricate sections, had to be measured and cut very precisely. This was done by using a pair of dividers. These could be set to a measurement on a plan or template, which could then be transferred to the stone.

A pair of dividers was the symbol of the powerful guild (association) of stone masons.

Dividers could also be used to scribe (score) a circle on stone

Spade end for laying and pointing mortar

The toothed end on this chisel was used to scrape away stone.

Lead weight for the plumb line

Straight walls
Castle walls were usually built absolutely vertical. To check that they were perfectly true, masons hung a weight on a cord, called a plumb line, down from the top of the wall. If the weight touched the wall at any point, it was not straight.

CROWBAR STONE CHISEL TROWEL CLAW CHISEL

12TH CENTURY (YELLOW)
13TH CENTURY (PURPLE)
CIRCA (ABOUT) 1300 (RED)
14TH CENTURY (GREEN)

Our castle changes
The castle featured in this book is based on Goodrich Castle in Herefordshire, England. It is set on a rocky cliff overlooking a river valley. The original timber and earth enclosure was replaced in about 1150 by a stone tower keep. Walls and towers were built around this in about 1205, and new inner buildings were constructed in 1300.

Marble
Easily obtained stone, such as granite, sandstone, or limestone, was used for most castle building. For finer interior work, masons might import more valuable marble, which was sawn into blocks.

Cutting and carving
Specialist craftsmen of all kinds were needed for the building of a castle. Besides an army of masons (shown in the picture right) there were carpenters who worked timber for joists, floors, and roofs; smiths who forged hinges, chains, and tools; plumbers who piped water and sewage; and engineers who diverted streams to create a moat.

The shape to be cut is marked out on the block.

Free masons shaped the stones.

A rough block of stone is trimmed smooth using a small axe or saw.

Banker masons carved the blocks into shape with mallets and chisels.

Stone that had been cut and smoothed was called ashlar. It was used on the outside of walls and for pillars.

Lime is slaked (burned) before it is used in mortar.

Index

Acknowledgments

The publisher would like to thank: Robert Graham and Angela Koo for research, Chris Bernstein for the index, Mary Atkinson for editoral assistance, Venice Shone and Peter Radcliffe for design help, and Lee Thompson from the picture library.

The publisher would like to thank the following for their kind permission to reproduce their photographs:
c=centre; t=top; b=bottom; l=left; r=right; a=above
Aerofilms: 7tr; The Ancient Art and Architecture Collection: Ronald Sheridan 19cla; AKG, London: 12/13b; The Bridgeman Art Library: Avila Cathedral, Castilla-Leon/Index:

46ca; Biblioteca Estence, Modena, Italy: The Sun God, De Sphaera (15th century) 19tc; Bibliotheque Inguimbertine, Carpentras/Giraudon: The Trial of Robert d'Artois, Nicolas Claude Fabri de Peiresc (1580-1637) 7cr; Bibliotheque de L'Arsenal, Paris: The Garden of Love, Loyset Liedet (1460-78) 36bc; British Library, London: 37clb; Chronicle of St. Denis 37br; Des Proprietez des Choses 46cl (below); From the Coronation of Richard II to 1387, Jean de Batard Wavrin (15th century) 43br; Histore Universelle 47c; Manuscript of Pentateugrul 36cl; Bibliotheque Nationale, Paris: 20tl; Antiquites Judaiques, Jean Fouquet (c.1425-80) 47b; The Battle of Villejuif, Jean-Baptiste Edouard Detaille (1848-1912) 45bc; Crusaders Bombard Nicaea with Heads, William of Tyre (c.1130-85) 28tl; De Claris Mulieribus,

Giovanni Boccaccio (1313-75) 21ca; Froissart's Chronicle 24tl, 24/25b, 25tl; A History of the Siege of Rhodes (1483) 44br; Pillage of Jerusalem, Antiochus (1089) 44tc; Vigils of Charles VII, Martial de Paris (1484) 44bc; Bibliotheque Royale de Belgique, Brussels: 26bl; Christie's Images: The Accolade, Edmund Blair Leighton (1853-1922) 19cra; Musee Conde, Chantilly, France/Giraudon: August / Tres Riches Heures du Duc de Berry 34tl; Livre de la Chasse, Gaston Phebus (1387) 40bl; October / Tres Riches Heures du Duc de Berry 34b, 35c; 12 Scenes of the Labours of the Year, P. de Crescens (c.1460) 38tl/cl/bl; National Maritime Museum, London: 45c; Private Collection: The Tower of Babel, Nuremberg Bible (1483) 46br; Victoria & Albert Museum, London: Akbarnama Mughal (c.1590) 45cl;

Yale University Art Gallery: The Capture of Atlanta by the Union Army, Currier & Ives (1864) 45cr (below); British Museum: 18bl; The British Tourist Authority Photo Library: Harvey Wood 7tl; The Board of Trustees of the Armouries: 31cr/br; CM Dixon: 41cr; English Heritage Photographic Library: 9tr, 10bl; ET Archive: 13tr, 21br, 38c, 39br/cla, 44tr/c/bl, 45tl, 47cr; Robert Harding Picture Library: 11tr, 36tl; Michael Holford: 21tl; Museum of London: 14br, 15bl, 39ca, 47ca/cl; Rex Features: 14cl (below); Turner 15cr (below); Spectrum Colour Library: 46bc; The Wallace Collection: 17br; Werner Forman Archive: Kuroda Collection, Japan: 45tr; York Archaeological Trust: 43tr
Jacket: Robert Harding Picture Library: front cover cl